STAGE FRIGHT

Jane Lawes

Illustrated by **Giovanni Pota**

OXFORD
UNIVERSITY PRESS

Letter from the Author

I loved drama and performing when I was at school. Being in a play or a dance show was always a special experience. To begin with, there were the rehearsals – learning my part, having fun with my friends and watching the show gradually come together, knowing that the audience was in for a treat when the big day came, as well as the excitement of finding costumes and making sets. Then there was the thrill of the performance itself; whether I felt overcome with stage fright or filled with joy – or, often, a mixture of both – there was no other feeling in the world like it. With a rush of adrenaline, I was up on the stage showing what I could do, and when it was all over, I wished I could do it again.

Now that I'm an author, performing is one of my favourite things to write stories about. I hope you enjoy reading this one!

Jane Lawes

Prologue

Nightingale Junior School, Year Six classroom. It's just after lunch. The class are sitting at their tables. Our heroines, Parnita and Nadira, are sitting right at the back, nervously anticipating the announcement their teacher is about to make.

Mrs Sharma:	I'm delighted to tell you that the star of our end-of-year play will be Parnita. You're the best actor in the class, Parnita, and I know you're going to do a wonderful job.
Parnita:	Thank you so much! I'll do my very best; I promise.
Mrs Sharma:	And the second biggest part is going to Nadira. I know I can count on you two to work well together – you're my dream team!
Nadira:	(*to Parnita*) This is going to be the best end of term ever!
Parnita:	I can't wait to get started.

Parnita put down her pen and looked out of the window. All that she needed now was for her wish to come true …

Chapter 1
The Fateful Decision

Parnita pushed through the door into a classroom full of chaos. Nothing unusual about that – after having the freedom to shriek and race around the playground on a gloriously hot, sunny day, no one liked the idea of coming back inside and just sitting still, especially when Mrs Sharma wasn't even here to do the afternoon register yet.

Today, though, the shouts and swirls of laughter were even more boisterous than usual and the low hum of gossip was rising to a frantic buzz. Everyone was on edge, waiting to find out what parts they'd be cast in for the Year Six end-of-year play. It was going to be *Alice in Wonderland* this year so there were lots of bizarre and exciting roles on offer.

Parnita went to sit with Nadira at the back of the classroom. She loved acting and performing, so she was keener than anyone to hear who Mrs Sharma had chosen for the star roles. Parnita was hoping to play Alice – she'd even imagined Mrs Sharma giving her the part when writing in her diary the night before. She believed she had the potential to be the star of the show. But she also had to admit that some of the other girls were just as good at acting, and Mrs Sharma might decide that one of them was best for the role. Even if she didn't get to be Alice, she thought, she'd settle for one of the other main parts – perhaps the Queen of Hearts or the White Rabbit.

Parnita's thoughts fizzed off in a million directions, while all around her the hubbub of multiple excited conversations escalated.

'I'm sure I won't get a speaking part,' said Alex, his voice rising out of a large group gathered at the front of the classroom. 'I was unbelievably rubbish in that *Twelfth Night* workshop last week. They had to ask me to speak up three times!'

'At least you didn't trip over your own feet right at the start. I hadn't said a single word before I fell flat on my face!' replied Ben.

Suddenly, one clear voice rose above the general clamour, claiming all of Parnita's attention.

'I really hope I get to be Alice,' simpered Ruby, flicking her auburn ponytail over her shoulder. Her friends all nodded and agreed obsequiously.

Parnita rolled her eyes at Nadira; Ruby's friends were just like sheep – always agreeing with what Ruby said and did, and altering their opinions to match hers. But Parnita knew it would be a challenge to beat Ruby to the role of Alice. Ruby took acting, dancing and singing lessons at weekends, and she was the most popular girl in their class.

'Watch out! You nearly knocked me over!' Ruby shouted as Robbie charged past her, chasing Finn around the room with an elastic band 'worm' intended for the back of Finn's neck.

Finn yelled and tried to scramble under one of the tables, and Robbie followed, tugging at Finn's shoe to hold him back. Ruby crossed her arms in annoyance, but Parnita and Nadira looked at each other and laughed. No one noticed Mrs Sharma as she stepped silently into the room.

'Robbie!' she thundered. 'Get up off the floor and give that shoe back to its owner! I've told you before – the classroom is not a climbing frame.'

Finn slithered guiltily out from under the table and reclaimed his shoe, and Robbie looked at the floor.

'Sit down, both of you,' said Mrs Sharma. 'Honestly, if you can't behave yourself in a classroom for five minutes, I don't know how you expect me to trust you with a part in the play.'

The class was quiet while Mrs Sharma busied herself with opening windows and taking the register.

Parnita tapped her foot impatiently under the table. She thought back to the *Twelfth Night* workshop, which they'd done the week before with a proper theatre company who had come into school for their class Shakespeare project. She'd loved every moment of it – learning from real actors and getting to perform part of an actual Shakespeare play – but she knew Mrs Sharma had been watching and using it as an audition for the end-of-year show. She'd tried so hard, making sure that every word was distinct, so that Mrs Sharma and Mr Ferguson (their class teaching assistant) could hear her all the way at the back of the hall. She'd put plenty of expression into her lines too. But had it been enough to get a part in the show?

Mrs Sharma finished the register and looked up at the class. Parnita felt as if cumbersome hippos were dancing ungracefully in her stomach. This was it: time to find out.

'I'd better tell you what parts you'll all be playing, hadn't I?' Mrs Sharma said with a smile.

Parnita gripped Nadira's hand under the table. She was desperate for Nadira to get a good part too, because it was the last school play they would be in together. From September, they would be at different secondary schools. This was the last term when they'd get to be partners in Drama and PE lessons, be able to spend every break time walking around the playground with their arms linked and be able to sit next to each other in assembly. This would be their last chance to revel in the excitement of rehearsing and putting on a show together.

'All of you will get a chance to shine,' Mrs Sharma said encouragingly, as if she could read Parnita's thoughts. 'Not everyone will have a big speaking part, but those of you who don't have a lot of lines will have dances and songs to learn, so you'll all get to show your parents what you can do.'

Nadira squeezed Parnita's hand under the table. 'Good luck!'

'You too!' Parnita whispered back.

'We've decided that our Alice will be Ruby,' announced Mrs Sharma.

'Yesss!' Ruby hissed, and her friends all grinned at her.

Parnita felt one of the dancing hippos fall down with a thump of disappointment.

'The White Rabbit will be played by Nadira,' Mrs Sharma continued.

Nadira gasped and turned to Parnita with wide eyes.

'Well done!' whispered Parnita. The only main part left for a girl was the Queen of Hearts. She swallowed hard and fixed her hopes on that.

'Ben will be our Mad Hatter, and Finn is going to be the March Hare,' said Mrs Sharma.

9

Finn cheered and waved his ruler in the air, and Ben and Alex whooped with laughter at the triumphant outcome of Ben's nearly-disastrous audition.

Mrs Sharma listed the remaining parts and who would be playing them – and Parnita's name still wasn't called out.

The remaining dancing hippos crashed to a halt. Did that mean she hadn't got a speaking part at all? Was she going to have to dance in the background with Robbie and the others who weren't nearly as interested in drama as she was? She looked over at Robbie, who was sprawling halfway across his table to high-five Finn. He didn't seem at all concerned that he didn't have a speaking part.

'Quiet, quiet!' called Mrs Sharma. 'I'm not quite finished. There's one more major part, and that's the narrator. For this role, we've chosen Parnita.'

Parnita looked up.

'You'll have to learn a lot of lines,' Mrs Sharma said. 'More than anyone else. But I know you can do it.'

Parnita nodded. She didn't trust herself to speak, feeling the burn of tears at the back of her eyes, knowing that all her hopes were crushed. The narrator wasn't a proper part. There wouldn't be any acting – no last great performance with Nadira – just reciting long screeds of boring lines to explain the story. How could Mrs Sharma have overlooked her like this?

'That's great!' said Nadira. 'Well done!'

'Thanks,' muttered Parnita.

Nadira looked so pleased and excited about being the White Rabbit.

Parnita forced a smile on to her own face, despite the frustrated almost-tears that were threatening to spill on to her cheeks. 'You're going to be so great, Nadira.'

'Do you really think so?'

'Of course!' Parnita replied with more enthusiasm than she felt. 'You're brilliant at acting. You'll be awesome.'

'I'll be so nervous! But I can't wait. I just wish you were going to be Alice instead of Ruby.'

'Me too.'

'The narrator's a really good part, though,' Nadira said, beaming. 'You'll be onstage the whole time. We will be acting together in our last play after all!'

Parnita nodded sorrowfully, not wanting to squash Nadira's happiness. What Nadira said was true, in a way. But it wasn't what she'd been hoping for. They wouldn't really be acting together – Nadira would be acting with Ruby. Parnita would just have to stand to one side and watch instead.

Chapter 2
The Most Important Role

Parnita took her school bag upstairs to her room and flopped on to her bed, her bright red and orange duvet welcoming her home with its cosy embrace. She dragged the *Alice in Wonderland* script out of her bag and began to read.

Mrs Sharma hadn't been exaggerating when she'd said Parnita had a lot of lines. There were reams and reams of them to memorize! She took a pink highlighter out of her pencil case and started to go over her part with it, making her lines spring brightly out of the page.

As she read, she couldn't help keeping track of Ruby's and Nadira's lines too. There was no denying it – their parts were infinitely more fun. Her mind raced away, picturing the bright and brilliant costumes the others would get, while she would no doubt be stuck in the universal narrator uniform of 'just wear some plain black clothes'.

Parnita finished reading through the play and threw the script aside grumpily. She didn't think that her narration was exciting or funny; none of it even seemed necessary – surely everyone knew the story of *Alice in Wonderland* already? She briefly contemplated whether her part had just been added as an afterthought to give her something to do. It was all so unfair! She was the one who always had a theatre trip as her birthday present, who fantasized about being a great actor or playwright when she grew up, and had books about scriptwriting on her bedroom shelves.

Suddenly she sat up. Even if her part in the play was boring, that needn't mean giving up on drama altogether. She fished a small silver key out of its secret hiding place and unlocked the drawer in her bedside table.

After a moment's rummaging, she found her diary. She opened it to a blank page, trying not to think about what she'd written yesterday. Now she would write about what had *actually* happened.

In the kitchen, just after home time. Mum is cooking a curry for tea when Parnita trudges in.

Parnita: (*glumly*) Hi, Mum.
Mum: (*brightly*) Oh, hello! I didn't hear you come in! How was your day at school?
Parnita: Dreadful.

Mum:	Why – what's happened? Is it—
Parnita:	(*interrupting*) Mrs Sharma handed out the parts for the play, and I've got to be the narrator.
Mum:	I'm so proud! When can we get tickets? I can't believe how grown-up you are now. I remember when you first started school, you were too shy to speak in front of the class – and now you're going to be the narrator in your last play at Nightingale Junior School!
Parnita:	It's not like I'm the star of the show or anything. Ruby's going to be Alice. The narrator's just about the most boring part you could possibly have.
Mum:	What about Nadira?
Parnita:	(*dully*) She's playing the White Rabbit. Even she got a better part than me.
Mum:	Nonsense! You know, I think the narrator is the best part of all. Do you want to know why?
Parnita:	(*muttering*) Sounds like you're going to tell me.
Mum:	Because being chosen to be the narrator proves that Mrs Sharma rates you as the best reader in the class. It shows she trusts you to learn all your lines, and to be onstage

15

	for the whole play without getting anything wrong, or misbehaving, or losing your confidence. I really think that it takes a special kind of person to be the narrator.
Parnita:	(*sighing*) But I don't want to be the special kind of person who always gets safe, boring jobs to do. I want to be the star of the show for once! Is that too much to ask?

Parnita put the book to one side. Clearly, it *was* too much to ask!

* * *

In PE the next day, Mrs Sharma and Mr Ferguson gathered the class in the hall, where dust danced in the streaks of sunshine coming through the windows.

'There'll be a big dance number when Alice first arrives in Wonderland,' explained Mrs Sharma, 'and all of you are going to be in it. Everybody find a space and we'll get started.'

Mr Ferguson led them though their usual PE warm-up and as they windmilled their arms around, Nadira leaned in to Parnita.

'At least we get to be in the dance together.'

'True,' Parnita nodded, but she didn't hold out much hope that this would make up for being the narrator while Nadira got the fun of becoming the White Rabbit. Parnita suspected dancing wasn't her strength and could already envisage the main characters up at the front of the dance, performing extra steps, while she was hiding at the back.

'Cheer up!' said Nadira encouragingly. 'This is going to be really fun!'

Mrs Sharma arranged them into lines and Parnita was pleasantly surprised to find herself placed on one end of the front row, next to Nadira. They began to learn the steps – it was a bit like a line dance, with lots of jumping and turning and stepping. Parnita had to concentrate hard on remembering the steps – some of which were distinctly silly. She noticed how effortlessly Ruby seemed to pick it up.

To begin with, Parnita felt self-conscious; dancing really wasn't her strength, and the exaggerated movements didn't make it any easier. But as Mr Ferguson and Mrs Sharma danced along with them, Parnita couldn't help getting swept along by their enthusiasm. Soon the whole class was throwing themselves into the routine as if nobody was watching, and Parnita reluctantly realized she was enjoying herself. There was one section where they were all paired up, twisting and twirling under each other's arms, and Parnita and Nadira were soon breathless with laughter at the effort of both twisting under simultaneously without getting stuck.

'Do you think this is going to look all right onstage?' Nadira wondered, after they'd just run through everything.

'As long as we don't mess it up,' muttered Parnita, reverting to her grumpiness once the music stopped. She was hot and uncomfortable with the exertion of dancing; the door was open to let in some air, but none of it seemed to be reaching her, and her T-shirt was clinging uncomfortably to her back.

'We've got ages and ages to practise before the performance,' Nadira replied, but Parnita thought that she seemed less excited than before. Was she worried about embarrassing herself in front of everyone?

'Oh well, at least we'll all look silly together,' Parnita sighed, rolling her eyes in mock despair.

'Let's go over it again,' Nadira said, her voice tinged with anxiety.

'Are you OK, Nadira?' It was Ruby, coming up behind them. 'I can help you go through the steps if you want.'

'Thanks!' said Nadira.

Parnita tried to catch Nadira's attention, but her best friend was already too busy concentrating on following Ruby's movements to see her.

* * *

Later that morning, Mrs Sharma announced that they were going to have their first proper rehearsal for the play.

'I'm going to start with the scene where Alice follows the White Rabbit. So that's Ruby, Nadira and Parnita. Mr Ferguson will take the rest of you back to the hall to practise the scene where the Queen of Hearts is playing croquet.'

Parnita and Nadira went to the front of the classroom to join Ruby while everybody else trooped out after Mr Ferguson. Nadira stepped closer to Parnita.

'You don't think I'm supposed to have learned my lines already, do you?'

Parnita heard that hint of nervousness in her voice again. 'Of course not! It's only the first rehearsal. Just focus on learning how Mrs Sharma wants you to act it out and I'm sure you'll be perfect.'

'Thanks, Parnita.' Nadira looked reassured and gave her a wobbly smile.

Mrs Sharma called them over to help shift some of the tables out of the way to make a mini stage area. She began by blocking out the scene, telling them their positions and movements. Parnita had the first lines of the whole play, but Mrs Sharma didn't want any of the narration added yet.

'Just sit there and wait for now,' Mrs Sharma said to Parnita. 'We'll go from your first line in a minute.'

Parnita settled herself on a chair at the front and watched Ruby and Nadira start getting into character.

The play started with Alice singing a song, and then chasing the White Rabbit across the stage; Nadira had to keep stopping to check her watch and then hurry on, so that every time Ruby was just about to reach out and catch hold of her, she jumped further away.

Parnita could see why Nadira had been cast as the White Rabbit; she was using her love of animals to make all her movements perfectly rabbity – twitching her nose and holding her hands up like delicate paws – and even without a costume it was obvious who she was supposed to be.

Parnita sat and watched as the scene gradually started to come together. It took much, much longer than the promised minute.

'Let's try it with your narration now, Parnita,' Mrs Sharma said at last.

But Parnita had only got halfway through her second sentence when Mrs Sharma stopped her to talk to Ruby and Nadira. It went on like that, over and over again.

'Am I doing OK?' Parnita asked, when they'd gone back to the beginning for about the tenth time.

'Perfect,' said Mrs Sharma distractedly. 'Just keep saying your lines while I figure out how Ruby and Nadira can make this scene look good.'

Parnita glared down at her script in frustration. For all that her mum had said the narrator was the best part, she felt like she might as well not be there at all.

* * *

'Oh! Parnita,' said Mrs Sharma, after what seemed like hours. 'Can you take this to the office for me, please? I didn't get a chance earlier and I'm on duty at lunchtime.'

Parnita slowly got to her feet and took the envelope Mrs Sharma held out to her, feeling almost glad to pass the remaining endless minutes until lunchtime with a meander to the office and back.

All the way there, she mused on the injustice of it all; getting an awful part in the play in the first place, then after she'd been told by Mrs Sharma and her mum that her part was in fact very important, no one was interested in letting her practise it! She walked as slowly as she could, carefully placing one foot in front of the other so that one heel was touching the toes of the other foot. She walked like that all the way along the corridor towards the office, but when she looked at her watch, she was surprised to see only two minutes had passed.

'Mrs Sharma asked me to bring you this,' she said to Miss Jenkins in the office. Miss Jenkins had a fan by her desk, whirring out a stream of delicious cool air, and Parnita shuffled as close to it as she could.

'Lovely! Thanks, Parnita,' said Miss Jenkins, taking the envelope. 'I hear you're going to be the narrator in our end-of-year play. Well done!' She was positively beaming. Parnita did her best not to scowl. 'You'd better get back to your classroom – it'll be lunchtime soon.'

Parnita strode back out into the corridor, and then slowed to a saunter again as soon as she was out of sight of Miss Jenkins's desk. She swung her arms and looked at the artwork on the walls – messes of brightly coloured paint by Reception and Year One, some pretty impressive illustrations of favourite book characters by Year Four, and her own attempt at drawing a bowl of fruit and some glass bottles amongst the Year Six contributions. She stood and looked at her drawing, next to Ruby's, which was much better than hers. *Annoying, perfect Ruby – always the best at everything.* At least she could look forward to a relaxing half an hour after lunch, walking around the playground arm in arm with Nadira, talking about anything but that morning's rehearsal.

Parnita quickened her step and returned to the classroom. But Nadira, Ruby and Mrs Sharma weren't there. Mr Ferguson was, shepherding a few stragglers towards the hall for lunch.

'Where's Nadira?'

'She and Ruby went off to lunch already,' said Mr Ferguson. 'Come on, the rest of you need to get moving too, before all the food gets snapped up by the early birds! Hurry up, Robbie!'

Parnita tagged along forlornly with Mr Ferguson and the group of boys. She scanned the lunch hall for Nadira, and eventually spotted her at a table with Ruby and her friends. There weren't any extra seats. Ruby was talking animatedly and Nadira was following her every move with an admiring smile.

'Move up!' said Robbie, poking Parnita in the back.

Embarrassed, she realized she was holding up the entire lunch queue.

Her tray loaded with spaghetti and salad, she looked around again. No, there was definitely no space near Nadira and Ruby. She felt suddenly completely alone, as if she'd been in a shipwreck and now she was stranded on a raft in the middle of the ocean. She always sat with Nadira at lunch – she had no idea what to do instead.

A horrible thought suddenly grabbed hold of Parnita. Nadira and Ruby were both going to the local girls-only school in September, while Parnita would be moving on to the same secondary school as Robbie, Finn and most of their class. What if next year it was Nadira and Ruby who were best friends? What if it was starting already? Parnita felt tears blurring her vision, and shook her head, angry with herself.

'Wakey wakey!' Robbie sang in her ear. 'There's an empty table over here.'

Parnita didn't know whether that was an invitation to sit with him and Finn, or if he was only trying to get her to move out of the way, but she followed him to the table anyway and sat down.

'Mr Ferguson said we could go back to the classroom this lunchtime and help him make some scenery and props for the play,' said Robbie. 'Want to come?'

'Maybe,' Parnita replied with a shrug. She was already sick of the play, but anything would be better than watching Nadira and Ruby laughing together.

Chapter 3
Hidden Hopes

When Parnita, Robbie and Finn returned to the classroom after they'd had lunch, Mr Ferguson had laid newspaper over the tables and was busily setting out paint palettes and brushes, cups of water and pots of shining, bright paint in fairground colours.

More and more people came to see what Mr Ferguson had planned for the set. Every time the door opened, Parnita hoped that Nadira would walk through it, but she didn't.

'We'll need lots of giant flowers for the scenes in Wonderland,' said Mr Ferguson. 'Can you lot make a start on those?' He handed Parnita, Robbie and Finn large pieces of cardboard. 'Use any colours you like. Make them as outlandish as possible!'

'At least Mrs Sharma is allowing us to make the scenery. I wish she'd let us help with the script or writing the songs, though,' Parnita lamented, when Mr Ferguson had walked away. 'We're the ones leaving to go to secondary school – it's supposed to be *our* last performance!'

Robbie and Finn nodded.

'Well, maybe we should ask her,' said Finn. 'I've got an idea for a dance we could include.'

The room filled with a babble of joyful noise as they got on with drawing and painting, and Mr Ferguson went around the room helping, advising and making everyone laugh. Only Parnita was quiet. She couldn't help wishing that Nadira was here, painting by her side. They could have made matching flowers, and that way the flowers they'd worked on together as best friends would be right there onstage for everyone to see.

'Look at mine!' said Robbie. His flower was like an optical illusion – he'd painted circles made up of lines of alternating colours, so that when you looked at it, it seemed to be moving.

'It makes my eyes hurt!' Parnita said with a laugh.

'Maybe it'll hypnotize the audience into thinking that dance we learned earlier doesn't look totally ridiculous.'

'I think we're going to need a lot more than your flowers for that!'

'Honestly – I've got a great idea for a dance,' said Finn. He put his paintbrush down, stepped back from the table, and started to demonstrate some moves.

Parnita and Robbie clapped and whooped. Finn had just dropped to the floor to try some more advanced spins when Mr Ferguson came over, waving his hands in the air with an expression of horror on his face.

'Not in the classroom!' he cried. 'You'll get paint everywhere!'

Finn stopped dancing and popped back up on to his feet, grinning.

'Can we choreograph a dance for the show?' he asked Mr Ferguson, taking up his paintbrush again.

'You'll have to ask Mrs Sharma,' said Mr Ferguson. 'Maybe if you practise a routine and show it to her, she'll include it.'

Finn pumped his fist in the air and spun around in another circle, forgetting that he had a paintbrush in his hand and very nearly swiping a line of bright red paint across Mr Ferguson's shirt and tie.

'Careful!' cried Mr Ferguson, leaping back quickly from the arc of the paintbrush.

'Alex said earlier that he wants to put something together. I'm sure he'll work on a dance routine with me!'

said Finn, plonking his brush into a pot of water and heading outside.

Parnita and Robbie continued painting for a while.

'I wish I had a speaking part in the play,' Robbie suddenly remarked after he had added some finishing touches to his swirls of mind-bending circles.

Parnita looked at him in surprise. She hadn't thought Robbie would be bothered by it in the same way that she was. He was always joking around and hadn't seemed to care at all when Mrs Sharma announced the cast.

'I think you'd have been great as the March Hare,' said Parnita. 'You're confident enough.'

Robbie shrugged, not making eye contact. He carried on painting. 'I'm not sure that Mrs Sharma thinks I'd take it seriously enough.'

Parnita focused on her careful brushstrokes, not certain how to respond. She wondered if it was true that Robbie wasn't seen as responsible by most of their teachers, but she would never have expected him to have cared.

'That isn't fair on you,' she said eventually. 'It's obvious you'd have been good at it.'

Robbie shrugged again.

Parnita wanted to say that she felt the same way about her own part – that it was horribly unjust and she would resent every minute of being the narrator – but suddenly she didn't feel she could.

'Wow, look at that!' cried Mr Ferguson, coming up behind them and pretending to boggle his eyes at Robbie's vivid flower.

'It's going to hypnotize the audience so they think the play is the greatest thing they've ever seen,' Parnita said, grinning at Robbie again.

'So I see.'

'Can we try it out on Mrs Sharma after lunch to see if we can hypnotize her into including a new dance in the play?' asked Robbie.

'Absolutely,' said Mr Ferguson with a wry smile.

'We'd better make some more!' said Parnita.

Mr Ferguson and Robbie both laughed and Parnita felt her mood lift. This lunchtime hadn't been so awful after all.

Chapter 4
Left Out

Nadira and Ruby came hurtling into the classroom just as Mrs Sharma began to look around to see if everyone was ready for the afternoon register.

'Sorry we're late,' said Ruby. 'We were right at the end of the playground when the bell rang.'

Nadira slipped into her seat next to Parnita. 'Where did you go after lunch? I was going to see if you wanted to come with us, but you'd disappeared.'

'I was here,' Parnita replied coolly. 'Some of us stayed in to make scenery for the play.'

'Oh.'

'I didn't think you'd want to,' Parnita lied. She knew Nadira loved art lessons and was excellent at drawing. 'You looked busy.'

'Oh,' Nadira repeated quietly, frowning slightly. 'I'm really sorry we didn't wait for you for lunch. Mrs Sharma hurried us out.' She was so earnest that Parnita had to believe her.

'That's OK,' she said, her annoyance thawing. 'I actually had fun. We started painting flowers for the Wonderland scenes!'

'I'll definitely stay in and paint with you next time.'

Parnita felt her whole body relax with relief.

* * *

The temperature inside the Year Six classroom crept up and up with every day that passed, and by the end of the following week, even the teachers were making paper fans to cool themselves down.

On Thursday morning, Mrs Sharma wanted to go through the Mad Hatter's Tea Party scene, which included Alice, the White Rabbit, the Mad Hatter and the March Hare – so that meant only Ruby, Nadira, Ben and Finn were needed. There was a bit of narration, and Parnita guessed she'd be sitting on the sidelines as usual, watching Nadira and the others enjoy themselves. But she was wrong – it was even worse than that.

'Everyone else, please go with Mr Ferguson and run through the scene at the Queen of Hearts's palace,' said Mrs Sharma. 'Parnita, you have lots of lines in that scene, so please join Mr Ferguson's group.'

Parnita and Nadira exchanged a forlorn glance at being separated, but Parnita had no choice but to join the rest of the class in traipsing over to the hall for their rehearsal.

Mr Ferguson set up chairs to mark where the edge of the stage area was going to be, and placed one chair on the 'stage' for Parnita to sit on.

There was going to be another dance in this bit of the play – one in which half the group pretended to play croquet using flamingos as sticks and hedgehogs as balls (Mr Ferguson promised convincing props by the performance) and the other half pretended to be gardeners, terrified of the Queen of Hearts and frantically painting the garden's white roses red.

Parnita sat with her script while the others learned the routine. However hard she tried to memorize her lines, she couldn't help being distracted. To everyone's amazement, Mrs Sharma had agreed to let Finn and Alex choreograph a new routine for the gardeners to perform in this scene. Finn was busy rehearsing the Tea Party scene, so the others were dancing without him now, but it still looked amazing.

Robbie stole the show, managing to make real comedy out of pretending to be afraid of the Queen of Hearts, while simultaneously performing the new dance routine perfectly.

Parnita couldn't help feeling a bit envious that he had transformed a non-speaking part into something extraordinary, but the dance was so good that jealousy was soon overcome by enjoyment. She actually laughed out loud once or twice, and Robbie caught her eye and grinned.

When Mr Ferguson ran the scene from the beginning, Parnita tried to use facial expressions as she spoke to convey shock and suspense, aiming to put just as much personality into her boring narration as there was in the gardeners' dance.

'Good job, Parnita!' Mr Ferguson called, when she came to the end of her longest speech almost without glancing at the script. 'You must have a great memory!'

Parnita sighed to herself. He didn't seem to have noticed that she was trying to act as well. She could have said her lines in a monotone and he'd probably have been just as impressed.

She slumped back in her chair and let the rest of the rehearsal roll on without her.

* * *

'How was your rehearsal?' Nadira asked as they joined the back of the lunch queue.

'All right.' Parnita deliberately didn't return the question; she didn't want to hear about all the fun Nadira had been having with Ruby. Clearly, though, Nadira wanted to tell her about it.

'I just can't remember any of my lines!' Nadira whispered anxiously. 'I'm never going to learn them in time.'

'We've got ages still,' said Parnita. She saw tendrils of steam rising and twisting into the air from a huge tray of shepherd's pie and, despite the hot weather, her stomach rumbled at the sight of it.

'I bet you know your lines already,' Nadira continued fretfully.

Parnita turned back to face her with the most encouraging expression she could muster.

'But I don't have any acting to do. You do – so just focus on that first and you'll pick up your lines as you go. I'm sure it won't matter if you get a few words wrong here and there, as long as you get the character right.'

'I don't know – ' Nadira hesitated, then added quickly, 'maybe you're right.' Her face wore a strained smile, and Parnita noticed that it didn't reach all the way to her eyes.

The rest of lunchtime didn't get any better.

As Parnita and Nadira were finishing lunch, Ruby appeared behind them and asked if Nadira wanted to go with her and a couple of the others to carry on practising the scene they'd been working on in the lesson.

To Parnita's horror, Nadira got up and followed Ruby out of the hall and Parnita couldn't think of a single thing to say to Nadira to make her stay, or a suitably biting comeback for Ruby. All she could do was sit and watch her best friend walk away.

* * *

'What's the matter, Parnita?' Mum asked that evening.

Parnita was sitting glumly at the kitchen table, gazing out of the window and ignoring the play script that was open in front of her. Shrugging, she made no reply.

'Do you still feel upset about being the narrator?' Mum prompted, sitting down at the table with her.

Parnita nodded. It was easier than explaining what was happening with Nadira.

At the end of lunch break, Nadira had returned to the classroom to sit next to Parnita and she had tried to be extra cheerful and complimentary about the flowers Parnita and Robbie had painted. But Parnita's annoyance had persisted. She hadn't wanted to hear Nadira say friendly things – she'd wanted Nadira to have chosen her over Ruby in the first place. So she'd been deliberately short in her answers, and eventually Nadira had stopped trying to make things normal again.

Parnita didn't want to talk about any of this with her mum – she felt like she might cry if she tried.

To remove any chance of crying over Nadira – and then having an explanation dragged out of her by her mum – Parnita took her script up to her room. But she didn't read it. She got out her diary and poured every bit of frustration from the day on to the page.

The school hall, at lunchtime. Parnita and Nadira are sitting at a table, having a lovely conversation. Ruby walks up behind them.

Ruby:	Hey, Nadira! We're going to go outside and do some more work on the scene we were practising before lunch. Do you want to come?
Nadira:	*(looking at Parnita)* Um …
Ruby:	*(with a sickly-sweet smile)* It's so nice and sunny out there! It'll be such good fun.
Parnita:	Nadira and I were just going to—
Ruby:	*(interrupting)* Come on, Nadira, we really can't do the scene without you! And you did say you wanted to work on your lines.
Nadira:	OK – let me just put my tray away!

Ruby smiles smugly, just like she did when she was chosen to be Alice in the play.

Nadira:	*(standing up)* Sorry, Parnita … I really, really need to practise …
Ruby:	Me too – I have so many lines to learn.
Parnita:	Well, if you need so much extra rehearsal time, maybe you shouldn't be playing Alice at all!

39

> *Ruby's smile fades and she storms out. Parnita is pleased with herself for thinking of a good comeback to put Ruby in her place, but Nadira leaves anyway, and Parnita looks sadly down at the table.*

Parnita looked at what she'd just written. Was it wrong to feel that way about Ruby? A little voice inside her whispered that perhaps she wasn't being fair. Could it be that she was a little bit jealous of Ruby? Parnita quickly pushed away the thought. None of this was her fault, she told herself. Ruby was the one who was coming in and interfering with everything. Anyway, she couldn't help how she felt about things. She couldn't make herself like Ruby. Could she?

Parnita had just put her pen down when there was a knock on her bedroom door.

'Come in,' she called.

'Hi,' said Dad, popping his head around the door. 'I've been thinking about your problem.'

'What do you mean?'

'I know you haven't got the part you most wanted,' said Dad, coming fully into the room and sitting down on the end of her bed. 'Is there anything you can do about it to turn it into a role you *do* want to play?'

'You mean change the script?' Parnita asked doubtfully.

'Perhaps,' said Dad. 'Or add some little touches of your personality to make it more yours. I always think narrators in stories can be great characters if they seem like real people.'

'That's what a really good actor would do, isn't it?'

'And you are a great actor,' said Dad. 'Remember when you wrote that play last summer, and you and Nadira and her brothers all performed it for us? These lines in the script are your starting point – it's up to you to make the narrator come to life.'

Parnita stared at her dad in amazement and her mind began to race with ideas for little touches she could add and extra jokes she could include.

'Thanks, Dad!' she said, grabbing her script and flicking through the pages, buzzing with enthusiasm.

'Are you feeling better?' he asked.

'Much better!' said Parnita.

As her dad left the room, she was already scribbling notes on the first page of the play. She was going to do just what he suggested – she was going to turn the narrator into the greatest part in the play!

Chapter 5
The Beginning of the End

Parnita had to wait until the next afternoon to really put her plan into action.

Nadira had been quiet all the way through registration and assembly. Parnita guessed that this was in return for the way she had responded to Nadira's cheerfulness with clipped, cold comments the previous afternoon. She made a few attempts to break through to Nadira's usual sunny nature, but it seemed like Nadira would rather read her script than say anything to Parnita.

In the morning they had lessons outside, sitting under the shade of a group of trees near the classroom. Usually this was a wonderful occasion where everyone enjoyed Mrs Sharma's classroom rules being relaxed, but this time, Parnita could only watch as Nadira plumped herself down on the grass next to Ruby, and she actually found herself wishing they were still overheating in the stifling classroom.

In a flash of anger, she decided that she wasn't going to beg Nadira to be friends again. If Nadira wanted to talk to her, she could make the first move. But it looked as if Nadira was either equally stubborn or that she genuinely wasn't bothered that Parnita wasn't speaking to her. Parnita hoped it was the first thing; the alternative was too awful to contemplate.

At lunchtime, Nadira and Ruby went over their lines together. Turning her back on them, Parnita saw Robbie and Finn dashing about with some of the others in a game of football.

'Can I play?' she asked them.

'Yeah!' called Robbie. 'You can be on my team.'

Parnita grinned as he kicked the ball across to her and she started dribbling it towards the goal.

Parnita was totally focused on the game until she was tackled by Finn, who won the ball and booted it back the other way. Parnita turned to follow it and caught sight of Ruby and Nadira again, their heads bent together over the script. Feeling the first sign of tears burning behind her eyes, she switched her attention back to the game and carried on running.

* * *

For all her grumbling, Parnita had to admit that the play was starting to look and sound really good, even if they had only started rehearsals a couple of weeks ago. Everyone had been working tirelessly to learn the songs and dances, and it was becoming clear how it was all going to fit together. Parnita had watched every part of it from her place at the side of the stage area and she felt the production's momentum carrying her along too, despite all her earlier misgivings. There were still various things that needed more practice – people were coming in and out at the wrong times, forgetting lines here and there, dancing precariously close to what would be the edge of the small stage, and Wonderland itself didn't look particularly full of wonder without any costumes or set – but now they were ready to start their first run-through of the whole play in the hall.

Parnita's imagination raced ahead of all the chaos of everyone getting into their places, to the actual rehearsal when she was going to make her part one that she'd actually enjoy playing. She'd spent all of the previous evening thinking about how she could weave in humour and gestures so that she wasn't just explaining a story that everybody already knew. She'd read articles and reviews of plays online and she was convinced that adding some comedy would improve Mrs Sharma's adaptation of *Alice in Wonderland*. Now it was time to show the rest of the class what she could do.

When Alice went to follow the White Rabbit down the 'rabbit hole', Parnita pretended to be horrified.

'Has Alice never seen a scary film?' she said to the audience. 'Someone needs to tell this girl – never follow a strange rabbit into a dark tunnel!'

Giggles fluttered across the hall and Parnita felt each laugh like a thumbs up.

'Stick to the script please, Parnita,' called Mrs Sharma irritably. 'We don't have time for messing about.'

Parnita felt a hot flash of shame. Everyone was looking at her – and even though some of them had been laughing at her jokes, now she felt they would all think she was trying to sabotage the play, when all she was doing was trying to improve it! It wasn't her fault the narrator's lines were too dull for words. But she didn't dare disobey Mrs Sharma, so she slumped back in her chair and looked down at her script while the others practised a song for what felt like the thousandth time.

She sensed someone nearby and looked up. It was Robbie.

'I thought that was really funny.'

'Thanks,' Parnita replied, relieved that at least one person had understood what she was trying to do.

'I guess Mrs Sharma just wants things to be the way

she's written them, so that she can check the script to make sure people are doing it right.'

'But my lines are so boring!'

'Better than having no lines at all.'

'I know,' said Parnita. 'Sorry.'

'It's OK. I really do think adding in some jokes would have made the play better.'

Parnita sighed. 'Well, now we'll never know.'

Robbie wandered back to his place on the other side of the hall as the song ended.

Robbie had been kind to tell her that he'd found her additions to the script funny, she thought. Maybe he could empathize because he was always getting in trouble for making jokes himself. But it would have made her feel a thousand times better if it had been Nadira who had come over to commiserate.

She tried to catch Nadira's eye, but she had her head buried in her script again, and Parnita could see her eyes scanning rapidly over the words, as if she were trying to cram them into her brain before they could escape. They were supposed to be best friends! If the situation were reversed, she liked to think she would have been by Nadira's side instantly, saying she thought her jokes were hilarious.

When the rehearsal got going again after the song, Parnita tried to muster some enthusiasm for her part, but it wasn't the same. The idea of giving the narrator some personality had been keeping her going all day, and now Mrs Sharma had shot it down.

Chapter 6
Heat and Ice

'How was school today?' Mum asked when she and Parnita were walking home.

Parnita shrugged and swung her rucksack by one of the straps so that it brushed in the dust on the hot pavement.

'Did you have a bad day?' Mum pressed. 'How did the rehearsal go?'

'Awful!'

Suddenly everything overcame her: the big emotional swing from feeling excited about her idea to the burning shame of being told off by Mrs Sharma; the fact that Nadira hadn't even tried to comfort her; the usual end-of-day tiredness; it all bore down on her. The humid day gave extra heat to her unhappiness, and it all came out as tears of frustration. She hated crying in public, but luckily they were far away enough from school that no one from her class was likely to see.

'What happened?' asked Mum.

'I tried what Dad suggested. I made up a joke and I added it to my lines. People liked it – they laughed! But Mrs Sharma got cross with me and told me to stop messing around.'

'Maybe she didn't understand why you were doing it. Have you told her how you feel about being the narrator?'

'No,' Parnita replied dejectedly. 'She'd just think I was being ungrateful.'

'You don't know that. Why don't you give it a try? If you explain to her that you think your part would work better with a little more personality, she might agree to change your lines a bit. I'm sure she only told you off because you hadn't prepared her for what you were going to do. After all, she's trying to run a class play – she can't have everyone just improvising their lines as they go along!'

'I guess not,' Parnita agreed. 'I just wanted to contribute my own ideas. It's our play too!'

When they got home, Parnita headed straight for her bedroom and the consolation of her diary. The rehearsal wasn't the only thing that had gone wrong that day. Sometimes it was easier to write down what had happened, rather than confiding in her mum.

The school hall, at the end of the rehearsal. Even though she's vowed not to make the first move towards being friends with Nadira again, Parnita's resolve has already crumbled and she's waiting by the door for her best friend.

Nadira approaches and they walk out of the hall together.

Parnita: That was probably the most boring rehearsal so far, which is really saying something.

Nadira is reading her script as they walk back to the classroom and doesn't say anything.

Parnita: I can't believe Mrs Sharma was so uptight about me adding a joke.

Nadira still doesn't reply, not even to say something comforting to her oldest and dearest friend.

51

Parnita: I was only trying to make the play better for everyone!

Still silence from Nadira. They've almost reached the classroom and she hasn't said a word.

Parnita: Are you actually ignoring me now?

Nadira looks up, finally, as if Parnita is the one being unreasonable.

Parnita: Whatever.

Parnita strides through the door into the classroom, annoyed with herself for running after Nadira and trying to make up, when clearly Nadira doesn't want to talk to her at all.

She brushed a few tears off her cheeks with the back of her hand as she finished writing. Then she threw the diary back in the drawer and refused to think about Nadira any more.

She decided to focus on the script instead and give it one more go, writing out her suggestions for jokes and changes properly this time. Then tomorrow she'd show

Mrs Sharma what she'd done – and if that didn't work, she'd resign herself to performing the role of the narrator the predictable way.

* * *

Parnita tapped her foot under the table in time with the tick-tick-tick of the clock on the classroom wall. It was almost break time, and that meant it was time to approach Mrs Sharma about changing her lines. But what if Mrs Sharma refused to listen to her, or she looked at her ideas for new lines and thought they just weren't good enough?

When the bell finally went, a surge of bodies pressed towards Mrs Sharma's desk, worksheets were thrust on to the table, and then another surge took them towards the door and the glorious sunshine outside.

Parnita hovered.

'Everything all right, Parnita?' Mrs Sharma asked as Parnita approached timidly.

'I wanted to talk to you about the play,' Parnita began.

'What about it?' Mrs Sharma asked as she shuffled the worksheets into a tidy pile.

'I'm sorry I added a joke without asking you,' said Parnita, launching into the speech she'd spent all morning rehearsing in her mind. 'I thought that I could make the narrator more like a character in the play, instead of just someone telling the audience what's going on. I thought it might be funny, and make things a bit more … entertaining – ' She trailed off towards the end of her sentence and held out the copy of the script that she'd written her notes on. 'I came up with some more ideas, if you'd like to see them?' she finished hopefully.

Mrs Sharma took the script and silently read the notes Parnita had added to the first page – some of these were little jokes in her lines, but she'd also added some movement for the narrator too, so that instead of sitting at the side the whole time, she would follow Alice as she chased the White Rabbit, eventually shrugging at the audience and jumping down the rabbit hole herself as if she had no other choice.

A surprised smile spread across Mrs Sharma's face. 'This is really interesting!' she said. 'Will you leave the script with me? I'll read it during break and let you know later on what I think.'

'Thanks!' said Parnita. She was so thrilled that she almost skipped out of the classroom into the warm playground. Then she ran to find Robbie.

'Guess what?'

'What?'

'I wrote some more jokes and stuff for the narrator,' said Parnita excitedly. 'And Mrs Sharma said she's going to read the script now and maybe I'll get to add them to my lines!'

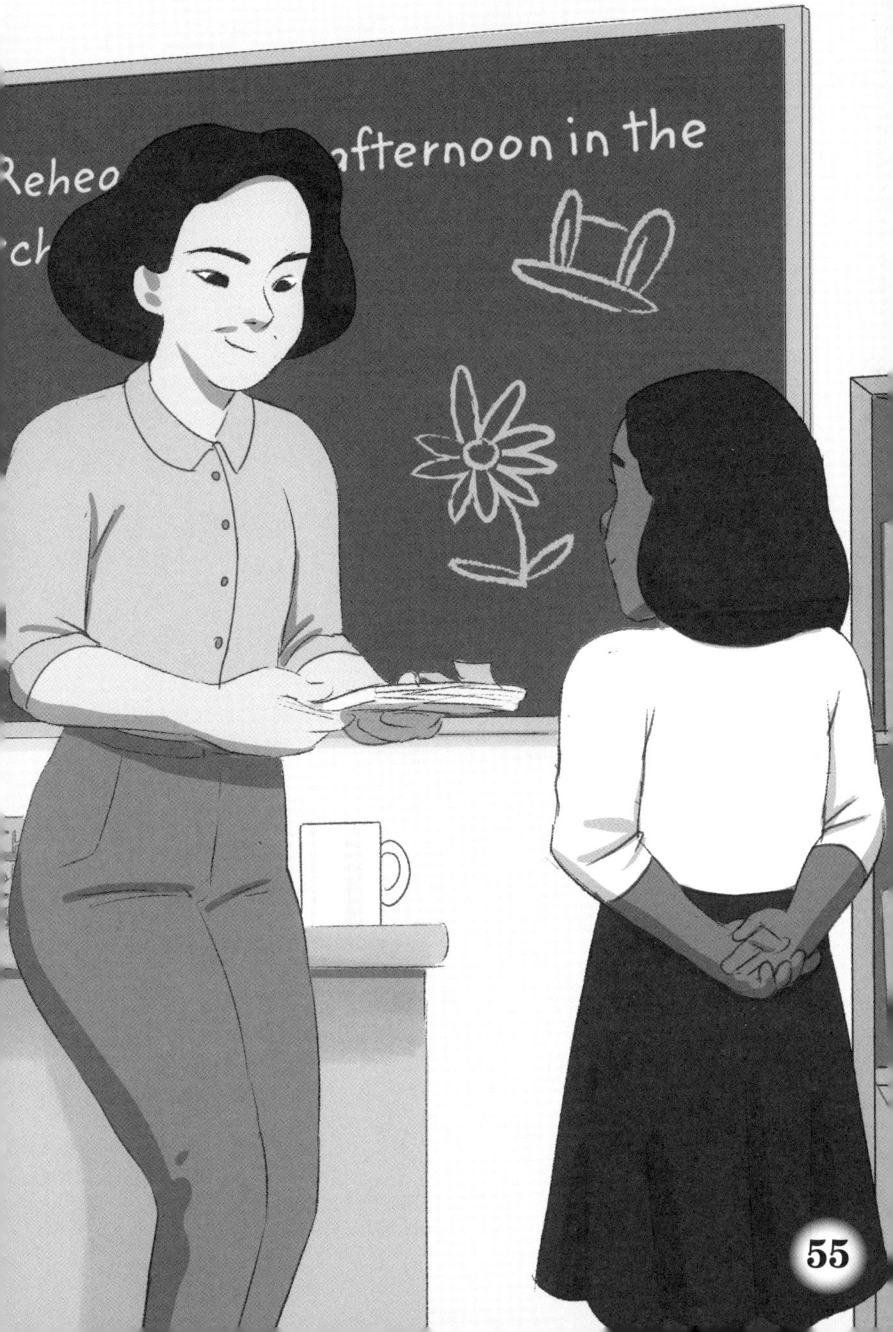
Reheo afternoon in the
ch

'But how will you remember it all in time?'

Parnita turned around and realized Nadira was standing just behind her, looking aghast.

'Will it change the lines the rest of us have to remember?' Nadira continued. 'How will we know when it's time for our lines if yours are different?'

Parnita stared at her. This was the last response she'd expected.

'Don't worry, Nadira,' Ruby said, suddenly reappearing at her side as if she'd popped out of a rabbit hole herself. 'You've still got ages to learn the new bits. And I can help you.'

But Nadira didn't seem to find that very reassuring. And neither did Parnita.

* * *

Parnita arrived back in the classroom uncharacteristically early at the end of break and Mrs Sharma was still sitting at her desk with Parnita's script in front of her.

'You've done a great job,' said Mrs Sharma. 'The jokes are funny, and I love all the physical comedy you've included. If you can act this out as well as you've written it, I think it's going to be a big success.'

Parnita felt her face heating up with pleasure at all her teacher's praise.

'I've made a few edits,' said Mrs Sharma. 'Have a read through and see what you think.'

Parnita took the script back, feeling excited that they were now collaborating on the production, just as she and Robbie had hoped. She sat back at her desk, and settled in to read Mrs Sharma's tweaks to her ideas while they waited for the rest of the class to come dawdling in.

Chapter 7
A Big Break

Parnita waited for that afternoon's rehearsal with a greater sense of anticipation than she had ever felt before. She hoped the rest of the class wouldn't think she was trying to take over the play, or that it was conceited to change Mrs Sharma's script. She wanted them to laugh at her jokes and made a silent wish that Nadira would laugh loudest of all.

'Parnita and I have reviewed the narrator's lines and we've made some changes,' Mrs Sharma announced at the beginning of the rehearsal, when they were all gathered in the hall. 'So don't be alarmed when her lines are a little different, or when she moves about the stage. Most of the time you just need to carry on as you were before – the joke is that the characters can't see the narrator, because she's from the outside world, looking in on them and commenting on their lives. OK?'

A murmur of consent rippled around the class. Robbie gave Parnita a big thumbs up, but Nadira's eyes were wide with surprise.

'I never thought Mrs Sharma would actually let you change the narrator's whole script!' she cried.

'Yes,' Parnita replied brusquely.

'That means I'm going to have to relearn all my cues.

I'd only just finished learning the old ones!' Nadira said in a panic-stricken voice. Tears filled her eyes and her cheeks were flushed.

'Nice one, Parnita,' Ruby muttered scornfully, putting her arm around Nadira's shoulders.

As Ruby led Nadira to her place, Parnita wondered why her oldest friend couldn't feel pleased at her achievement. This was going to make the play better for everyone. Why couldn't Nadira see that?

'OK, starting places, everyone!' called Mrs Sharma, and Parnita made her way to the stage area.

Gone was the narrator's chair. She didn't need to sit on it like an unnecessary observer any more. She was going to be right in the middle of the action!

Parnita knew that Robbie was on her side, and most people had looked pleased when Mrs Sharma had said she'd be adding jokes, but the expression of contempt that Ruby had given her ate away at her confidence. What if this was a really terrible idea after all and she was going to humiliate herself in front of the whole class, and then in front of all their parents?

The rehearsal started with a song and afterwards Alice chased the White Rabbit across the stage – creeping, stopping, reaching out and missing every time. Parnita stood to the side and rolled her eyes at the "audience", miming looking at her watch.

'This is Alice,' she said, pointing at Ruby. 'She's trying

to catch this smartly-dressed white rabbit, but she's going about it all the wrong way.'

Everybody giggled, apart from Nadira, but Parnita tried to ignore that and focus on everybody else's positive response.

Next the White Rabbit disappeared into the 'rabbit hole' by pretending to jump off the back of what would be the stage, followed by Alice. Parnita strolled over to where they had disappeared and peered down, then turned to shudder at the audience.

'No way,' she said. 'Absolutely not.' She paused. 'But if I don't go, you won't get to know what happens next.' She pretended to consider her options. 'Oh, all right!' she said finally. She squeezed her eyes tightly shut and jumped into the 'rabbit hole', as Ruby and Nadira had done.

Mr Ferguson and Mrs Sharma started clapping and soon everyone else joined in.

Parnita felt delight spread through her whole body, from her long black hair to the tips of her school shoes. She bobbed her head in a joking bow and laughed as she took up her place for the next scene.

* * *

'That was amazing!' Robbie said as he and Parnita wandered back to the classroom after the rehearsal.

Parnita smiled at him.

'My mum and dad will be really pleased when I tell them about today's rehearsal,' she said. Then she caught sight of Ruby and Nadira chatting ahead of them, and that chipped away at her until the happiness that she'd started to feel about the play began to fade.

'Parnita,' said Mrs Sharma, when she and Robbie got back into the classroom. 'What do you want to do about your costume? I was just going to ask you to bring some plain clothes from home, but that doesn't seem right now that the narrator is a proper character. Do you have any ideas?'

'Can I think about it over the weekend?' Parnita asked, thrilled to be consulted like this and especially pleased that her additions to the script meant she could avoid the much-dreaded Boring Narrator Costume.

'Of course,' said Mrs Sharma. 'I'll have a think too and we'll put our heads together on Monday.'

Parnita grabbed her school bag from her table and followed the rest of the class out to the playground where they waited for their parents at the end of the day. She was scanning the crowd for her mum when Nadira and Ruby walked past her together.

'I can't wait for you to meet my dog, Rory!' Nadira was saying.

'Oooh, I love dogs!' Ruby gushed.

Parnita couldn't believe it – was Ruby going over to Nadira's house? Parnita had been playing with Rory since he was a puppy; she hated the thought of Ruby fussing over him and having fun with Nadira and her brothers the way Parnita had been doing for years.

She caught sight of her mum waving at her from the gate where she was chatting to Nadira's dad, so she started walking towards her, which meant that, although they didn't realize it, she could still hear Nadira and Ruby's conversation.

'We can play with Rory out in the garden,' said Nadira. 'But let's practise for the play first. I want to make sure I don't forget all those new cues.'

'Of course I'll help you,' said Ruby. 'I don't get why Parnita wanted to change so many of her lines. She had loads to learn as it was.'

Parnita felt rage stirring up inside her at that remark. It was easy for Ruby to put up with learning the boring lines

Mrs Sharma had given her – she already had the best part in the play!

'I don't think she really wanted to be the narrator,' said Nadira. 'That must be why she's been acting so weird lately about you and the play and everything.'

Parnita didn't hang around to hear any more – she strode past Ruby and Nadira towards her mum. It was bad enough that Nadira was spending her Friday evening with Ruby, but now they were gossiping about her too!

Why was I so worried about what would happen between me and Nadira when we change schools in September? Parnita thought grimly. *It's happening already, and it's only June!*

Parnita's stride was rapid and unrelenting; she didn't even slow down when she reached her mum, but just faked a big smile and carried on walking out through the gate. Parnita's mum had no choice but to stop chatting to Nadira's dad and follow.

Chapter 8
Ice Builds and Heat Rises

One of the worst things about Nadira giving her the silent treatment on Monday morning – and Parnita giving it right back – was that they had to sit next to each other all through English and Maths, remembering every ten seconds that they weren't talking.

Parnita kept thinking of little moments from the weekend that, ordinarily, she would have shared with Nadira. But Nadira didn't even speak when they were checking their answers, and Parnita resolved not to break the silence either. She'd be more than happy to make up – but only if Nadira apologized first.

At the beginning of break time, as dark clouds began to gather over the classroom, Ruby came over to their table.

'Shall we practise that scene we were working on at your house?' she said to Nadira.

'Good idea!' Nadira replied.

Nadira followed Ruby to the door, then suddenly glanced back. She looked conflicted, as if she might be about to ask Parnita to come with them, but Parnita quickly looked away. She wasn't going to give Nadira or Ruby the satisfaction of seeing how hurt she was that they were going off together. She was still much too angry to make up.

She dawdled around the classroom while everybody else went outside.

Mrs Sharma was gathering up all the scenery that Parnita, Robbie and the others had made.

'What are you doing with all that?' Parnita asked.

'Mr Ferguson and I are going to set up the stage properly,' said Mrs Sharma. 'It's about time we had a rehearsal with all the scenery and props we're going to be using! Could you carry these across to the hall for me, please?' She handed Parnita a stack of brightly painted flowers and giant playing cards. 'Let's get all this into the hall as quickly as possible – it looks like there's a storm brewing!'

* * *

Mr Ferguson was already in the hall adding the scenery to the bare stage that had just been put up, with Robbie helping. Finn was off sick and Parnita realized Robbie was in a similar position to her, lacking his best friend and at a loss for how to spend break time.

The stage was made up of huge wooden boards that slotted together to make a platform about two feet off the floor, and took up one end of the hall. There was space on either side and Mr Ferguson had set up some screens in these spaces to create 'wings' – areas at the side of the stage so that people could remain hidden when they were offstage. His plan was to cover the screens with the painted flowers and the playing cards, and he set Robbie and Parnita to work pinning them up.

'Are your parents coming to see the play?' Robbie asked.

'Yeah,' said Parnita. She bent to pick up another flower and didn't try to continue the conversation. Her mind was so full of everything that she wanted to say to Nadira and all the things she wished Nadira would say to her, there just wasn't enough room to think about making jokes with Robbie.

'Mine too. I wish they'd get to see me playing a main part instead of just dancing around at the back.' Robbie had his back to Parnita so she couldn't see his expression.

'They'll still be proud to see you performing,' Parnita tried to reassure him, while driving a pin firmly into the top of a flower, pressing down hard with her thumb. At least she could take out some of her frustration on the scenery.

'You seem a bit down today,' Robbie observed. 'You've had a real result. Everyone thinks the narrator is the best part now!'

'It's not that,' Parnita said quietly.

'Are you and Nadira not friends any more?'

Parnita stared at him in amazement. How was it possible that Robbie had realized what was upsetting her when no one else had guessed?

'I don't know,' she said, her voice breaking down almost to a whisper. 'I'm not sure she wants to be friends any more.'

'You've been best friends forever!'

'But now she only wants to hang out with Ruby.'

'Maybe there's another explanation,' suggested Robbie. 'Something you don't know about.'

'A secret?'

'Or something she doesn't know how to talk to you about. Like how you didn't tell her that you didn't want to be the narrator, because you wanted to seem like you were happy for her being the White Rabbit.'

'You noticed that?'

'I just like chatting to everyone,' Robbie said with a

laugh. 'I end up finding out lots of things about people that way. Usually it's the *way* they say things, not *what* they say, that reveals how they actually feel.'

'I had no idea how clever you really are,' Parnita replied.

Robbie smiled a little resignedly at her and shrugged, pinning the last flower to the screen.

They stepped back to look at their work. The stage looked ... exactly as it did before: a wooden platform in the drab school hall, just covered with a few bits of painted cardboard. To say it was underwhelming was an understatement.

'What do you think?' asked Mr Ferguson, coming over to join them.

Parnita and Robbie looked at him, and their expressions said it all.

'You're right,' said Mr Ferguson. 'It needs ... something more. Leave it with me!'

Miss Jenkins, the school receptionist, popped her head around the door then and held out a piece of paper to Mrs Sharma.

'I just spoke to Finn's mother and she asked me to give you this message,' said Miss Jenkins.

'Thanks,' said Mrs Sharma, taking the paper. She read it and her brow creased with worry. 'Finn has had to go to hospital to have his appendix out! His mum says he's OK, but he won't be able to perform in the play next week after all.'

'Oh no!' exclaimed Parnita.

'Poor Finn! But ... what are we going to do about the play?' asked Mrs Sharma.

Parnita and Robbie looked at each other and Parnita gave him a nudge with her elbow.

A moment later, Robbie took a deep breath and stepped forward.

'I could play the March Hare.'

'Really?' Mrs Sharma frowned, and Parnita's heart went out to Robbie – Mrs Sharma looked extremely sceptical!

But Robbie persisted.

'Really,' he said, confidently. 'I know all the lines. I definitely think I could do it.'

'I don't know. It's a big responsibility.'

'I'll practise really, really hard every single moment until the play.' Robbie looked more earnest than Parnita had ever seen him before.

'I think he'd be great!' she chimed in. 'I'll help him rehearse.'

There was a long pause, and Parnita studied Mrs Sharma's face, trying to see what her decision would be.

'OK,' she relented. 'You can do it and we'll see how the next rehearsal goes. You've got to take it seriously, though, Robbie! Any messing around and I'll pick someone else.'

'I won't let you down,' said Robbie. 'I promise!'

'Good.' The bell rang for the end of break and Mrs Sharma hurried out.

'Thanks for backing me up,' Robbie whispered to Parnita, as they followed Mrs Sharma back to their classroom.

'You deserve it,' Parnita whispered back. 'I think you'll be the best March Hare there's ever been!'

She felt awful for Finn, knowing how devastated she would be if she was too ill to take part in the play, but she was glad that Robbie was going to get his chance to shine after all. She just hoped he hadn't been lying when he said he already knew all of the March Hare's lines, because he was running out of time to learn them – the performance was only a week away!

Chapter 9
Thunder and Lightning

Almost all of the next week was taken up with rehearsing for the show.

To everyone's excitement, Mr Ferguson had turned up at school with a full lighting and sound system, including coloured lights, a disco ball and a pair of huge speakers. He explained that he'd borrowed all the equipment from his friend, who was a DJ. The whole class was excited about the amazing lighting their play would now have, and secretly impressed that Mr Ferguson might actually be quite cool outside school.

Everyone had gained confidence and they were now working together and loving every moment of it; the new dance looked amazing, Parnita was throwing herself into the role of the narrator with all the personality and sparkle she could give it, and Robbie was proving to be a better March Hare than anyone had expected.

The only person who didn't seem to be having a good time was Nadira. Parnita noticed that she was messing up her lines more and more with every rehearsal. Mrs Sharma had to prompt her from the script all the time, and Nadira seemed frazzled and tired.

The storm that Mrs Sharma thought was coming still hadn't arrived; the air felt hotter than ever, the grass in the playground was scorched a pale dusty yellow, and it was impossible to sleep at night. But the atmosphere between Parnita and Nadira was icy and even though she desperately wanted to be friends again, Parnita didn't know where to start.

* * *

On the day of the performance, Parnita woke up with the urge to dance already running through her. They were going to perform the play for the rest of the school as a dress rehearsal before throwing open the doors of the hall to all their parents and relatives that evening. All lessons were abandoned in favour of fixing last-minute costume disasters, locating missing props, frantic run-throughs of songs and dances, and making sure the stage was perfectly set for the performance.

To distract herself from her worries about Nadira, Parnita had spent the last week making accessories for her costume with her dad's help. She'd decided to wear a T-shirt and jeans so that the audience would see her as 'one of them', but she'd found an old straw hat at home and had used a bright red ribbon and some glue to jazz it up with things that suggested elements of Wonderland: a playing card, a tag on which she'd written 'Drink Me', a little plastic flamingo and some paper flowers.

She'd also made some 'disguises' to put on and off at various points in the play when she was moving around the stage – her favourite was a costume of playing cards made out of two large pieces of cardboard, held together at the top by two pieces of string so that she could put it on over her head and have one playing card on her front and another on her back, and painted to show the Six of Diamonds and the Four of Clubs. She was so pleased with this that at the weekend she had persuaded her dad to make another one shaped like a giant teacup so that she could hide during the Tea Party scene.

Later that morning, Parnita was helping Robbie with his last-minute panic over the March Hare's lines, while Nadira and Ruby were huddled together in the opposite corner of the classroom. Parnita tried to swallow down her bitterness, but even when she turned her back on Nadira and Ruby, she was still painfully aware of them and was itching to know what they were talking about.

The classroom grew dark, as black clouds pressed down menacingly outside. Everybody jumped and squealed as lightning flashed outside the windows.

'Parnita!'

She turned and saw Ruby coming towards her with an anxious expression.

'You've got to come and help!'

'What's the matter?'

'It's Nadira! She's having a total meltdown about the play. She says she can't remember any of her lines! Please come and help. You're her best friend! You're the only one she'll talk to.'

'I don't think she wants to talk to me.'

'She does!' Ruby insisted. 'She's really panicking. I think it's stage fright. She's been worrying about performing the play for weeks.'

Suddenly, Parnita realized how self-absorbed and blind she'd been – all this time, Nadira had been genuinely afraid that she wouldn't be able to perform her part in the play, and Parnita hadn't even noticed. She'd been so involved in her own jealous feelings about Ruby and the play that she hadn't been there for her best friend when Nadira really needed her. She felt horrible.

Another flash of lightning illuminated the classroom. Everyone gasped and turned to the windows, waiting for the boom of thunder that came a few seconds later.

The icy feeling that had gripped Parnita's heart for the last week melted away at once and she followed Ruby across the classroom to the corner, where Nadira was curled up as small as she could make herself, with her back against the classroom wall and her knees pulled in to her chest.

Parnita found herself sitting on the floor next to her oldest friend. Another dagger of lightning ripped through the sky and more thunder rumbled behind it.

'I'd better go and get my costume on,' Ruby said.

Parnita smiled up at her gratefully; Ruby didn't seem so bad after all. In fact, when it really mattered, she was proving to be unexpectedly thoughtful.

'What's up?' Parnita asked Nadira. 'Ruby said you were worrying about the play.'

'I can't do it!' Nadira raised her head from where she'd been hiding her face in her knees and Parnita saw that her cheeks were marked with tears. 'I've forgotten everything!'

'I bet you haven't forgotten really. You've got stage fright. It probably even happens to mega-famous film stars. You just need to relax.'

'I can't relax! I can't do it!'

'OK,' said Parnita, scrabbling around in her mind for an idea that might help. 'Why don't we try taking some deep breaths? I'm nervous about performing too. I said that to my dad this morning and he showed me how to do deep breathing to control my nerves.'

'OK ... ' Nadira sounded extremely dubious about plain and simple breathing as a cure for stage fright.

'Copy me.' Parnita took a long breath of air through her nose and into her lungs, keeping it going for as long as she could, then slowly breathed the air out through her mouth.

Nadira followed her lead, watching her closely. They did a second long breath, and a third, and then Nadira broke into teary giggles.

'We must look so silly!' she said.

Parnita giggled too, and squeezed her best friend's hand gently.

'Do you feel any better?' Parnita asked.

'A bit. Mostly because you're here. I hated us not speaking to each other this whole time.'

'Same,' said Parnita. 'I'm sorry.'

'I'm sorry too. I'm sorry about the times I went off with Ruby without you. I was just so worried about being ready for the play that I didn't think about anything else, or that you might feel like I was abandoning you.'

'That's OK. I shouldn't have got in such a huff about Ruby going to your house,' said Parnita. It felt so shameful to admit that she'd been envious, but not being friends with Nadira had felt even worse. She took in another deep breath and then the words she'd been trying to hold inside came tumbling out.

'I was jealous of Ruby because she's Alice in the play, but I was also jealous that she was becoming friends with you. I know you're going to be at the same school as her next year, and I got really anxious that you'd like her more than me, and then you and I would stop being friends and we wouldn't have any more movie nights or go to each other's houses at weekends or have dance contests with your brothers – which are all of my favourite things in the world!'

'Oh Parnita!' Nadira exclaimed, throwing an arm around her and pulling her in for a sideways hug. 'We'll always be friends! Ruby's become a good friend but she's not you – no one could ever replace my best friend. I never meant to make you feel like that. I should have told you what I was worrying about all along.'

'And I should have told you what I was upset about. I can't believe I got so wrapped up in trying to make my role bigger that I didn't realize how stressed you were about yours,' said Parnita.

'Let's never have secrets from each other again,' said Nadira.

'Deal,' Parnita agreed. She turned and pulled Nadira into a proper hug.

'If you're not in your costume, you need to start getting ready immediately!' called Mrs Sharma, and Parnita and Nadira got up from the floor just as the first few drops of rain began to spatter against the windows.

'Are you going to be OK?' Parnita asked.

'I think so,' said Nadira. 'Deep breaths.'

The raindrops fell faster outside, bouncing up out of

the puddles that were quickly forming. The air felt fresher already.

'I think you'll be fine,' said Parnita as she pulled on her costume. 'Better than fine – I think you'll be brilliant! The best White Rabbit the world has ever seen.'

'And you're going to steal the show as the narrator,' said Nadira. 'I really like how you changed your part. You've definitely made it your own.'

'Thanks,' Parnita smiled. Even though loads of people had told her they liked her jokes, none of those compliments meant as much as hearing it from Nadira, her best friend.

Suddenly she didn't care so much about whether or not she was the star of the show. She and Nadira didn't need this to be their triumphant last performance together, because it wasn't the last of anything.

Chapter 10
Curtain Up

Parnita peeked out around the side of the screen – one of the ones she and Robbie had decorated with flowers – and watched as the Year Two children filed into the hall, their shoes dripping rainwater on to the floor, and sat down in front of the stage. The teachers had decided that Reception and Year One might not want to watch the whole play, so the audience was made up of Years Two, Three, Four and Five, sitting on the floor as they did in assembly, along with their teachers and teaching assistants, who had chairs along the sides of the hall.

The stage was bright and brilliant, with flowers and playing cards all over the screens at the sides and even bigger cards all along the front of the stage. The coloured lights, operated by two of their classmates with the help of Mr Ferguson's friend, were set up in a pattern of greens and blues for parts of the play set in the real world, and would later change to bright reds, oranges and pinks for Alice's adventure. It looked so inviting that Parnita wanted to step right into Wonderland and never leave.

Behind her she could hear the buzz of excitement and apprehension that everyone was feeling.

'Where's my hat?' Ben whispered, suddenly realizing he was missing the key part of the Mad Hatter's costume.

'What comes after the jump and then the turn?' someone else asked anxiously, marking through dance steps in the small space behind the stage.

'Shh, we're nearly starting!' whispered Ruby.

'Looking for this?' Mr Ferguson said to Ben, brandishing a very large top hat. 'You left it in the classroom!'

Handing the hat to Ben, he continued shepherding the parent who would be acting as sign language interpreter to his place at one side of the stage.

'Why did I volunteer for this?' Robbie asked Parnita in a whispered wail.

'Because you know all the lines and you want to show everyone what you can do,' said Parnita, sounding a lot more confident than she felt.

Inwardly, she was wondering a similar thing: why had she made her part much more complicated than it needed to be? Every joke seemed like an opportunity for the audience to sit in silence instead of laughing, pointing out to her that she should have just said the lines Mrs Sharma had written for her.

'What if no one thinks I'm funny?' she whispered. She wished she could tell Nadira how she was feeling, but her best friend was waiting in the wings on the other side of the stage and was too far away to provide any reassurance.

'*I* think you're funny,' Robbie said firmly. 'And I'm the class joker, so I should know.'

Parnita grinned. 'I've learned from the best.'

'So have I,' Robbie replied. 'Let's go out there and show them what great actors we are!'

Parnita raised her hand for a high five, and Robbie slapped her palm enthusiastically just before Mrs Sharma hissed, 'Quiet!' and gave the pair of them a disapproving glare. Robbie moved into position.

'Ready?' Mrs Sharma whispered to Parnita and Ruby. They nodded and stepped up on to the stage.

The play began with Ruby wandering around the stage in a daydream, singing a song about how much she wished for an adventure. Parnita pretended to watch her curiously, occasionally giving an exaggerated nod to show the audience that she agreed that Alice's life was very boring indeed.

All of the angry and jealous thoughts she'd had about Ruby in the last few weeks disappeared. She had to admit that Ruby's singing voice was sweet and tuneful, and that she was performing the song far better than Parnita could have done.

She remembered how concerned Ruby had been when Nadira had stage fright and how she had come straight to Parnita for help. Nadira was right – Ruby was a good friend after all.

The song finished and Nadira hopped on to the stage as the White Rabbit, fussing about being late and springing across the stage in comical bunny hops, moving just out of Ruby's grasp every time she got close.

'This is Alice,' said Parnita, making sure her voice was clear and loud enough to carry all the way to the back of the hall where Mrs Sharma was watching closely, making notes on everything that would need to be improved for the real performance. 'She's trying to catch this smartly dressed rabbit, but she's going about it all the wrong way.'

The audience erupted into giggles. Parnita could see that Nadira was trying not to smile too, and their eyes caught for a tiny moment, exchanging silent messages of confidence, before Nadira hopped away down the 'rabbit hole' at the back of the stage.

Now that the first moments of anxiety were over, Parnita relaxed and she enjoyed herself more and more with every minute that passed. The audience were hysterical when she ducked into her teacup disguise and looked out at them over the rim with a finger pressed to her mouth. She revelled in their laughter, but her focus was all on the stage – Robbie was about to make his first proper appearance as the March Hare.

Parnita bobbed down into her teacup as Robbie and Ben came on to the stage and sat down at a little table piled high with plastic food. Ruby came skipping on to the stage and Parnita stuck her head out from the teacup to say in a stage whisper, 'Alice stumbled upon the strangest tea party she'd ever seen.' She peered over at the table.

'She's right, it is strange! I've never been to a tea party where all the food is plastic!'

At the table, Robbie pretended to take a bite from a sandwich, then looked at it in exaggerated confusion when it turned out to be made of plastic. He launched into the first of the riddles that he and the Mad Hatter bombarded Alice with in this scene, and Parnita, who'd heard the script so many times now that she knew almost all of it by heart, held her breath as he rapidly recited the whole thing perfectly. She grinned to herself behind the teacup and really hoped that Mrs Sharma had also been impressed.

The new dance during the croquet scene was another big highlight. The choreography looked even better under the flashing disco lights and the audience went wild, clapping along in time with the loud music and cheering for so long when the dance finished that the dancers all had to take two bows before the play could continue.

By the time they got to the end of the show, everyone was ready to throw themselves into the final song and dance with all the enthusiasm they had. If anything, Parnita felt even more energized than before they'd started – she really thought she could do the whole play again right now if she was asked to – and as she and Nadira danced side by side, she saw the joy all over her friend's face and guessed that she felt the same way.

Robbie looked like he was having the time of his life too, and Parnita was delighted that he'd finally got his moment in the spotlight, and that he'd been noticed by Mrs Sharma for the right reasons at last.

'That was fantastic!' Mrs Sharma cried as the rest of the school trooped out of the hall afterwards. 'You are all stars. I can't wait for your parents to see it!'

Everyone started to gather up discarded props and costumes and put the set back the way it should be for the beginning of the play.

'Well done, Parnita,' Mrs Sharma said, coming over to her. 'I'm so proud of you – you took on a part that wasn't really the one you wanted and made it something special. You're a talented writer – and a great actor too! Your secondary school will be lucky to have you.'

'Thanks,' said Parnita. She was smiling so much that it almost ached.

'You know, Victoria Road School has a great reputation for drama. You must join their drama club next year. They have a writing club too – this time next year you might be writing your own plays!'

'I hope so!' Parnita replied. She'd been excited to see Victoria Road's drama studio when she'd been to look around, but her enthusiasm had been tempered by the thought of the looming separation from Nadira. Now she felt a renewed excitement about all the opportunities that might lie ahead in the future – a proper stage to act on, a writing club and a drama club, new friends and the chance to show the world what she was capable of creating …

'Robbie!' Mrs Sharma called, while Parnita drifted off into a dreamland. 'That was brilliant! I'm sorry I ever doubted you. You're going to make your parents very proud tonight.'

'Did I make *you* proud?' Robbie asked with a cheeky grin.

'You certainly did,' laughed Mrs Sharma.

Parnita heard this and bounded over to Robbie to exchange high fives again.

Nadira and Ruby came racing over and Nadira barrelled into Parnita with a hug while Ruby gave them both a big grin and then jumped in for a group hug.

'That went so well!' Nadira said to Parnita. 'You were totally awesome.'

'You were absolutely perfect, too. Stage fright? What stage fright?' said Parnita.

The hall was emptying out now. Parnita linked her arm through Nadira's and they walked back to their classroom together.

* * *

91

That evening, after the storm had washed the sticky, fractious heat away, a watery sunlight crept around the gaps in the blackout blinds.

Mrs Sharma finished her introduction, the audience applauded and then they fell quiet in anticipation.

Parnita and Ruby grinned at each other for good luck. After everything that had happened, Parnita now had an overwhelming feeling that she and Ruby – and Nadira and Robbie and everyone else – were on this stage together, working as one team to create something brilliant. Every unkind thought she'd had towards Ruby was forgotten – all she wanted now was for the play to be a triumph.

Parnita stepped on to the stage and took up her position at the side. She risked a quick glance out at the audience and she saw her mum and dad sitting in the fourth row from the front with Nadira's parents and brothers. Ruby walked on to the stage and began to sing.

Before Parnita immersed herself completely in her own special narrator character, she took one last look at her family in the crowd of parents. She couldn't wait to make them proud.

* * *

The final performance, right at the end. The whole class is onstage in character. Parnita steps forward as the narrator.

Parnita: After the adventurous day she'd had, when she finally got home, Alice was understandably very tired. She lay down, just for a moment ... and a second later she woke up. Had it all been a fantastical dream? It's what you might expect at the end of such a story. And maybe it was. But ... hang on – what's that?

Parnita points to something on the floor beside Ruby. Ruby holds up the White Rabbit's watch.

Parnita smiles and shrugs at the audience. She turns and walks to the back of the stage and jumps down the rabbit hole just before the lights go off.

The audience explodes into applause. The cheering continues until the lights come on again, and everyone stands onstage to take a bow. Mrs Sharma steps on to the stage and the audience falls quiet.

Mrs Sharma: Well done, Year Six, what a brilliant performance! They've all worked so hard to put on this show for you and I'm incredibly proud of each one of them. However, there are two people I'd like to say a special thanks to. Robbie – you took over the role of the March Hare at the last minute when Finn was ill and you've really proved to me what a star you are. And Parnita – I think it's safe to say this play wouldn't be what it is without you.

(*The class laughs.*)

Mrs Sharma: I'm really proud of the way you rose to the challenge of being our narrator. When I cast you in the role, it was because you're a good reader – I had no idea how wonderfully you'd bring it to life.

The audience claps and cheers again. Robbie and Parnita grin at each other. Nadira throws her arm around Parnita's shoulders and the lights fade to black.

95

Top Tips for Performing

1. Remembering lines can be difficult and everyone learns best in different ways. You could try recording your scenes with a friend so you can listen to yourself saying the lines, or making posters for your bedroom with the words you find hard to remember written out in bright colours. Or you could try to turn it into a game!

2. Look up. If you're looking down at the stage, the audience can't see your expression or hear what you're saying. Even if you feel shy, do your best to keep your eyes up – it makes you appear more confident!

3. Speak up. If you have a speaking part, ask a friend or your teacher to sit in the last row of the audience and practise saying your lines loudly enough so that they can hear you from the back of the room.

4. Spend some time thinking about how your character feels. What is making them say the things they're saying or do the things they're doing? If you're performing a dance or a song, think about the mood and style of the piece – is it joyful? Melancholy? Angry? Contemplative?

5. Have fun! If the audience can see that you're having a good time, they'll enjoy the performance more too. And remember: take a deep breath and smile!